# SCHIRMER'S LIBRARY
## OF MUSICAL CLASSICS

# PETER I. TCHAIKOVSKY

Op. 71a

# The Nutcracker Suite

Miniature Overture
March
Dance of the Candy Fairy
Russian Dance, "Trepak"
Arab Dance
Chinese Dance
Dance of the Reed-Flutes
Waltz of the Flowers

Library Vol. 1359
**Arranged for Piano, Four-Hands by**
**E. LANGER**
Edited by
CONSTANTIN STERNBERG

Library Vol. 1447
**Arranged for Piano Solo by**
**STEPÁN ESIPOFF**
Edited by
CARL DEIS

# G. SCHIRMER, Inc.

DISTRIBUTED BY
**HAL•LEONARD®**
CORPORATION
7777 W BLUEMOUND RD P O BOX 13819 MILWAUKEE, WI 53213

# SUITE
## For Full Orchestra
### Selected from the music of the Ballet
# "The Nut-Cracker"
#### by
#### P. I. TCHAIKOVSKY
#### Op.71
## Miniature Overture

Edited by
Carl Deis

Arranged for 2 hands by
Stepán Esipoff

30537

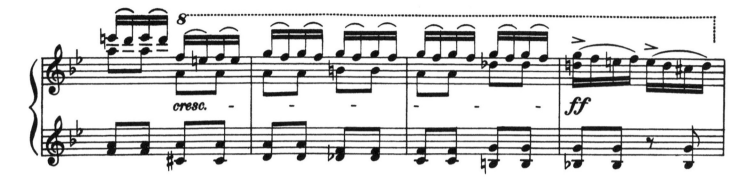

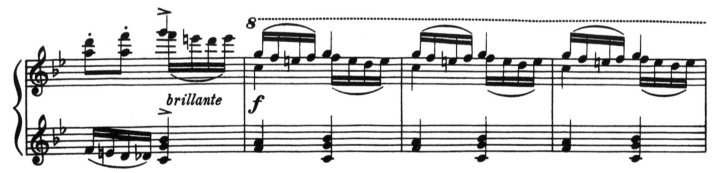

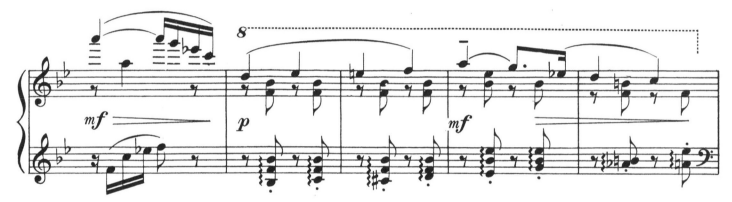

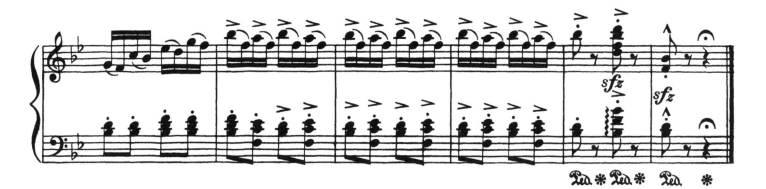

# March

Tempo di Marcia vivo

# Dance of the Candy Fairy

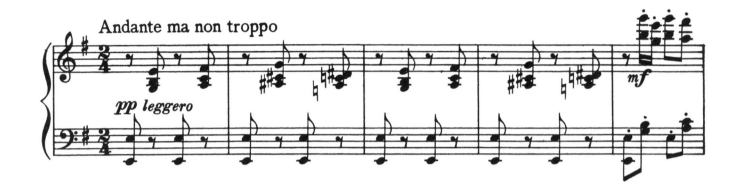

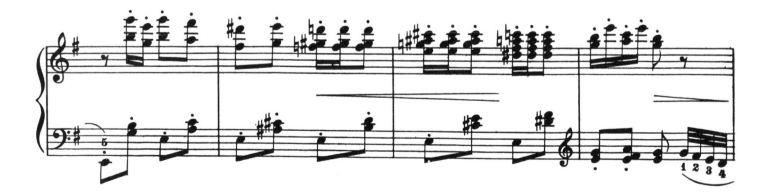

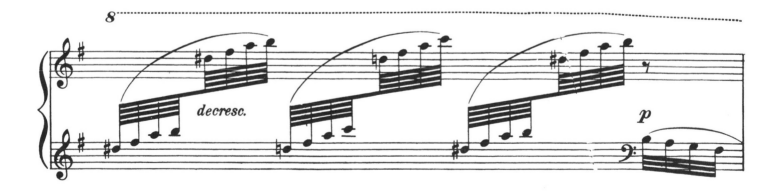

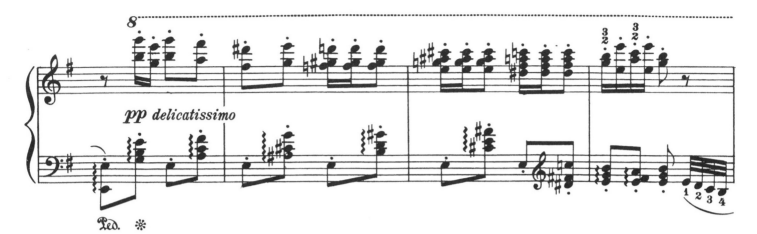

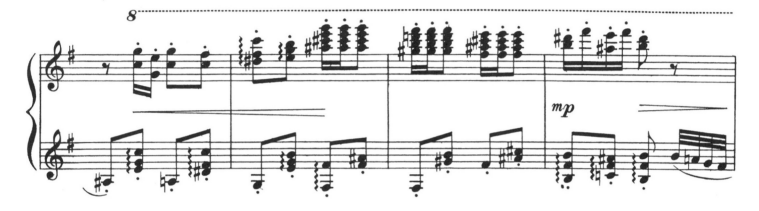

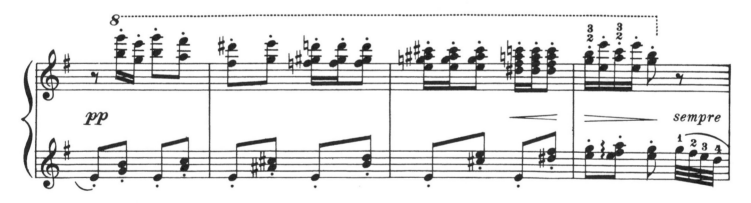

# Russian Dance, "Trepak"

Tempo di Trepak, molto vivace

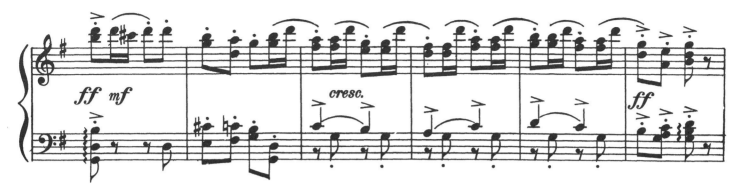

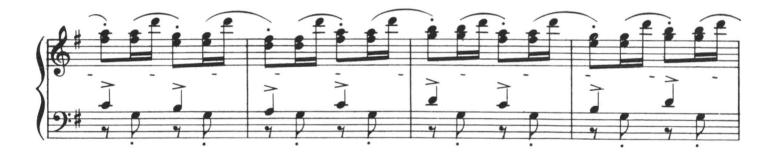

Prestissimo

# Arab Dance

Allegretto

# Chinese Dance

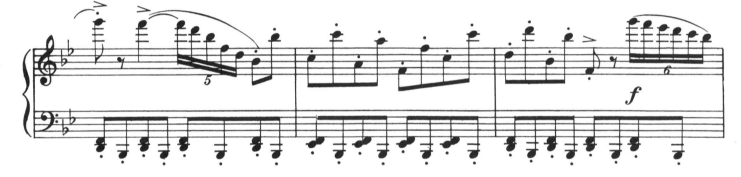

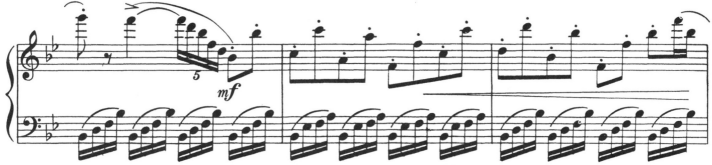

# Dance of the Reed-Flutes

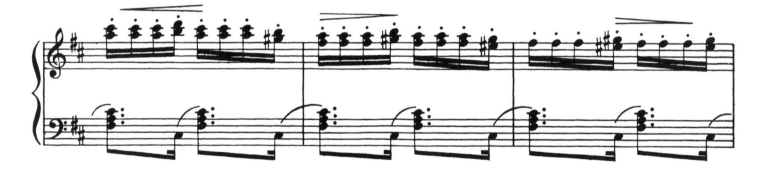

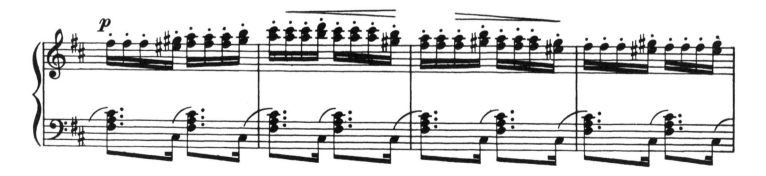

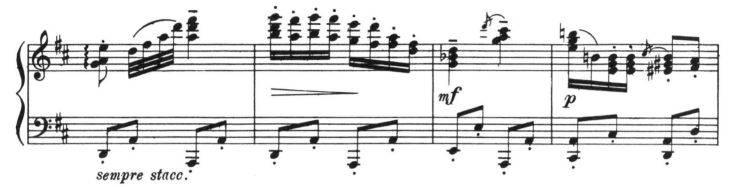

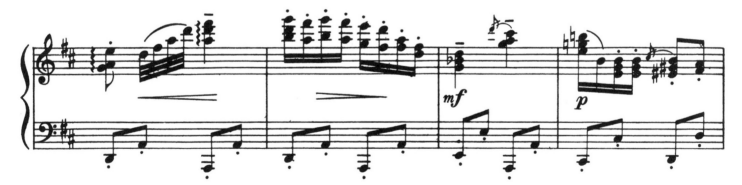

# Waltz of the Flowers

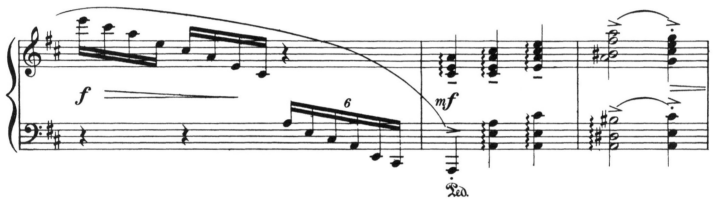

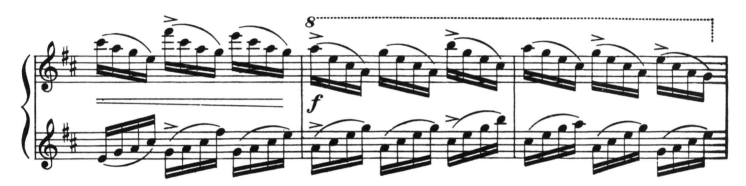

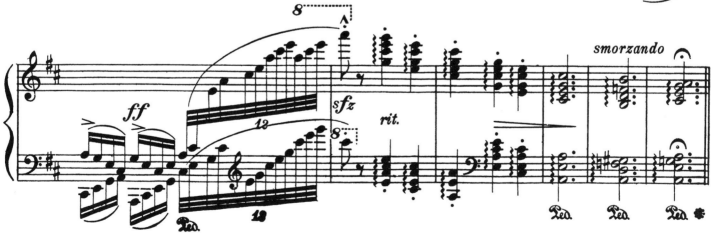

Con anima

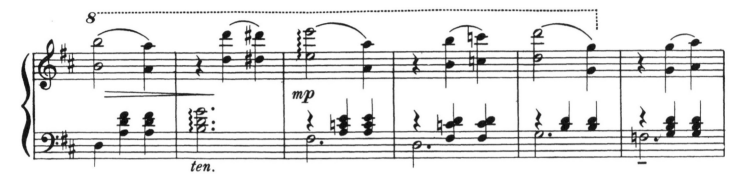

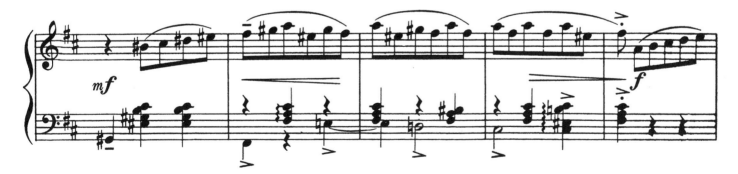

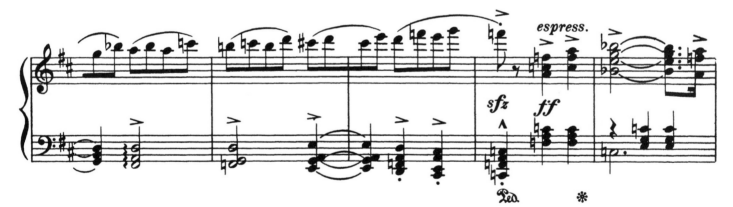

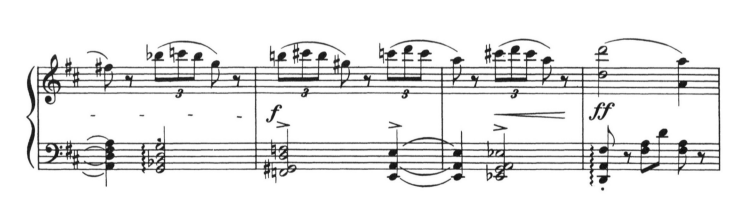

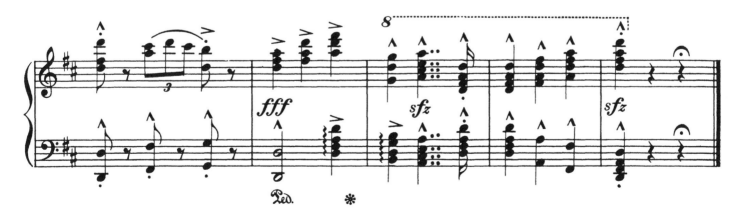